Moonshine
Cocktails

MOONSHINE Cocktails

THE ULTIMATE COCKTAIL COMPANION FOR CLEAR SPIRITS AND HOME DISTILLERS

PAUL KNORR

Quarry Books
100 Cummings Center, Suite 406L
Beverly, MA 01915

quarrybooks.com • quarryspoon.com

© 2015 by Quarry Books
Text © 2015 Paul Knorr

First published in the United States of America in 2015 by
Quarry Books, a member of
Quarto Publishing Group USA Inc.
100 Cummings Center
Suite 406-L
Beverly, Massachusetts 01915-6101
Telephone: (978) 282-9590
Fax: (978) 283-2742

www.quarrybooks.com
Visit www.QuarrySPOON.com and help us celebrate food and culture one spoonful at a time!

10 9 8 7 6 5 4 3 2 1

ISBN: 978-1-63159-107-5

Digital edition published in 2015

eISBN: 978-1-62788-767-0

Cataloging-in-Publication Data is available

Design: Ashley Prine

Cover Image: courtesy of Warren Street Books

Printed in China

CONTENTS

———— ✳ ————

INTRODUCTION

———————— ✳ ————————

MOONSHINE FINALLY SEES ITS DAY IN THE SUN

Moonshine, hootch, white lightning, un-aged corn whiskey—the names conjure up images of Prohibition-era gangsters and illegal backwoods stills. But a new face is being put on moonshine as a fresh crop of distillers emerges who pay their taxes and offer their wares in liquor stores and bars across the country. Even prime-time TV is getting in on the act. The Discovery Channel has *Moonshiners*, featuring real illegal stills in operation, and the History Channel has *White Lightning*, featuring the Hatfields and McCoys making moonshine together.

The appeal of moonshine has always been a part of America's history, and this recent surge in popularity should not come as a surprise, since it ties in to a trend in the foodie world that has been growing for years. The focus on eating locally produced, minimally processed products is a trend, and there is no better, more minimalist expression of the distiller's art than moonshine. There can be no artificial flavors or caramel coloring to hide behind, just as there can be no long aging process where the by-products of poor distillation can be masked by charred oak. Moonshine is the spirit as it comes directly from the still and must sink or swim on the skills of the distiller and the ingredients put into the mash. Add together a long, rich history, a localvore mentality, and some recent changes in federal and state laws, and you have the makings of a moonshine renaissance.

The history of moonshine in the United States is as old as the country itself. Many people don't know that the first civil war in the United States was not North versus South, but President George Washington versus a group of distillers in southwest Pennsylvania. What became known as the Whiskey Rebellion started in 1791, when Treasury Secretary Alexander Hamilton

George Washington and his troops preparing to suppress the Whiskey Rebellion.

instituted a tax on distilled spirits as part of his program to fund the debt from the Revolutionary War. Many of the people resisting the new tax were veterans of the war against the British and felt that taxation without representation was one of the principals they had fought against. The still owners used violence and intimidation against the federal tax officials that Washington sent until 1794, when Washington dispatched an army of 13,000 to enforce the law and restore order. The episode proved that the newly formed federal government had the willingness and ability to enforce its laws, but even then the tax was never really paid in full. The Pennsylvania distillers simply began to hide most of their production, paying taxes on a small portion of it but moving most of it into the woods and distilling by the light of the moon—moonshining.

After the Whiskey Rebellion, home distilling was a practice that went into hiding, never stopping completely, but faded from public view. Even after Thomas Jefferson repealed the tax in 1801, moonshiners remained hidden but could still be found wherever there was enough demand. The men and women on the American frontier have always prided themselves as being independent and self-sufficient and were resentful of anything that smacked of government meddling. Moonshining was—and is—an open secret within the isolated communities of the American West and in the Appalachian Mountains. In some of these communities moonshine can be used for barter and trade, and it has become part of the fabric of life there—hidden but as unremarkable as the gas station or the barbershop. It would not be until the institution of another ill-considered act of government that moonshine would once again come into the public eye.

The U.S. government outlawed the sale, production, importation, and transportation of all alcoholic beverages in 1920 under the Eighteenth Amendment to the Constitution. This was much worse than President Washington's simple tax on distilled spirits. The amendment allowed for a set of laws called the Volstead Act to be enacted that dictated an outright ban of all alcohol in the country and started what was to be known as Prohibition. Remarkably, Prohibition was popular with the public at the time it was first proposed and was actually successful in cutting the country's consumption of alcohol by at least 50 percent. In hindsight it seems obvious, but with shell-shocked soldiers back from World War I and no social safety nets available, it was not as easy to see that the benefits might not outweigh the unintended consequences of the new law.

Speakeasies, moonshining, rum-running, and bathtub gin were all brought to the public consciousness as a result of Prohibition. The newspapers and newsreels were filled with stories of gangs and raids and of the destruction of illegal liquor. Demand from the public was still there and, in fact, was so high that producing spirits or illegally importing them was a job that was becoming too big for any single band of outlaws. Criminals began to join forces, bringing together different groups with different areas of expertise to supply the big cities like Chicago and New York with the liquor that the people wanted. There were criminals that oversaw the moonshine production, those who oversaw the rum-running, and others who were responsible for the speakeasies and various aspects of distribution. All of these smaller operations reported to a central figure or family, giving rise to what was coming to be called organized crime. Crime bosses like Al Capone and Bugs Moran became household names, and the government seemed to be helpless to stop the violence when they would clash over turf.

Prohibition ended in 1933, with the Twenty-First Amendment, which repealed the Eighteenth Amendment. It was as much the Great Depression that forced the end of Prohibition as it was the rise of organized crime and the ensuing public outcry. The United States needed the tax revenue that the legal sale of alcohol would bring in, so even though Prohibition was repealed, a new set of laws that regulated and taxed alcohol took its place. These new laws affected the public only a little bit by way of higher prices, but they hit the producers and distributers harder. The laws passed after Prohibition required the licensing and taxing of all alcohol producers and regulated how distilled spirits could be sold, prohibiting distilleries from selling directly to the public.

Today, most people think of moonshine as a product of questionable purity made in the woods on cobbled together equipment by some hillbilly. Drinking it might make you blind or even kill you. It is true that there are some bad 'shines out there, and some illegal backwoods distillers are cutting corners and making an unsafe product. As anyone who buys illegal moonshine will tell you, you should never buy it from someone you don't know. There are many hazards that a bad, illegal moonshine can have for those drinking it. Ethylene and lead are poisons that can come from either the plumbing or from old car radiators that are sometimes used to cool the vapors from the still. Methanol can cause blindness and is sometimes added by unscrupulous distillers to boost the strength of their finished product. These are risks only associated with illegal, homemade moonshine. The new crop of moonshine distillers that you find in the liquor store are licensed and inspected. They produce a safe product that has all the mystique, flavor, and punch of moonshine and, since they paid their taxes, they are legally in the clear.

Starting in 2009, it was the desire for tax money that brought changes to the post-Prohibition laws allowing for the legal sale of moonshine in many states. For example, in New York, there is the Farm Distillery law that allows for production of small batches of spirits to be sold directly to the public. The catch is that the majority of the raw materials have to be from New York State. The result has been an explosion of new micro-distilleries all across the state, with a corresponding growth in the production of the fruits and grains that the distilleries need. It is laws like this one in New York and in other states that have made legal moonshine not only possible but profitable. One advantage that moonshine has over aged whiskey is that a craft distiller can start selling it right away, without having to wait years for it to age. While they store some moonshine in charred oak casks to age, distillers still bring in some money and show off their skills with their un-aged whiskey.

Moonshine can stand on its own straight out of the jar, but for some it may seem too harsh. Many traditional recipes exist for flavored moonshine if the straight stuff is too intense for someone. The most popular flavored 'shine is Apple Pie, where slices of apple and a cinnamon stick are added to the mason jar during the "bottling" stage. Some recipes for apple pie moonshine date back more than one hundred years. Other popular flavors include locally available fruits and berries such as peaches, blueberries, and blackberries.

Moonshine is an amazing spirit produced by innovative and motivated artisanal distillers. As the recipes in this book show, moonshine works wonderfully as the foundation for some exciting cocktails. These cocktails enhance its raw appeal and trade on the history and traditions of this most American of spirits.

Some Popular Brands

＊

Arkansas Lightning: Rock Town Distillery, Little Rock, AR

Benjamin Prichard's Lincoln County Lightning: Prichard's
    Distillery, Kelso, TN

**Buffalo Trace White Dog (Mash #1, Wheated Mash,
    and Rye Mash):** Buffalo Trace Distillery, Frankfort, KY

**Catdaddy Spiced Moonshine and Junior Johnson's Midnight
    Moon:** Piedmont Distillers, Inc., Madison, NC

Dark Corner Distillery Moonshine: Dark Corner Distillery,
    Greenville, SC

Death's Door White Whisky: Death's Door Spirits,
    Middleton, WI

Firefly Moonshine: Firefly Distillery, Wadmalaw Island, SC

Glen Thunder Corn Whiskey and White Pike Whiskey: Finger
    Lakes Distilling, Burdett, NY

High West Silver Whiskey OMG Pure Rye: High West
    Distillery & Saloon, Park City, UT

Hudson New York Corn Whiskey: Tuthilltown Spirits,
    Gardiner, NY

Kings County Distillery Moonshine: Kings County Distillery,
    Brooklyn Navy Yard, Brooklyn, NY

Ole Smoky Tennessee Moonshine: Ole Smoky Distillery, LLC,
    Gatlinburg, TN

Onyx Moonshine: Onyx Spirits, East Hartford, CT

The Drinks

82 QUEEN HONEYSUCKLE FIZZ

✳

1½ OZ. (45 ML) DARK CORNER HONEYSUCKLE SHINE
½ OZ. (15 ML) SIMPLE SYRUP
½ OZ. (15 ML) LIME JUICE
3 OZ. (90 ML) SPARKLING WINE

In a cocktail shaker filled with ice, combine the moonshine, simple syrup, and lime juice. Shake and strain into a champagne flute. Top with the sparkling wine and garnish with a lemon twist.

Johnny Williams, 82 Queen Bar, Charleston, SC

BEE STING

✳

½ OZ. (15 ML) FRESH LEMON JUICE
1 TBSP. (15 ML) HONEY
1½ OZ. (45 ML) MOONSHINE
4 OZ. (120 ML) SWEET TEA

In a Collins glass, add the lemon juice and honey and stir until the honey is dissolved. Add the moonshine, fill the glass with ice, top with sweet tea, and stir. Garnish with a lemon wheel or a mint sprig.

BEE'S KNEES

✳

1½ OZ. (45 ML) MOONSHINE

½ OZ. (15 ML) FRESH LEMON JUICE

1½ OZ. (45 ML) ORANGE JUICE

½ OZ. (15 ML) SIMPLE SYRUP

Shake all with ice and strain into a cocktail glass.

BERMUDA MOON SWIZZLE

✳

2 OZ. (60 ML) MOONSHINE

1 OZ. (30 ML) ORANGE JUICE

1 OZ. (30 ML) PINEAPPLE JUICE

1 OZ. (30 ML) CRANBERRY JUICE

2 DASHES ORANGE BITTERS

Shake all with ice and pour into a highball glass.

BERRY DEADLY

✳ ────────────→

8 OZ. (240 ML) MOONSHINE

I PINT (225 G) FRESH STRAWBERRIES

8 OZ. (240 ML) ORANGE JUICE

8 OZ. (240 ML) CRANBERRY JUICE

I CUP (½ PINT) ICE

In a blender, combine all ingredients. Blend until smooth and serve in a hurricane glass; makes 2–3 drinks. Garnish with an orange and cherry spear or a strawberry.

BITTER SAGE

✳ ────────────

2 LARGE SAGE LEAVES

½ OZ. (15 ML) FRESH LEMON JUICE

½ OZ. (15 ML) AGAVE SYRUP

1½ OZ. (45 ML) DARK CORNER MOONSHINE
   CORN WHISKEY

I OZ. (30 ML) RUBY RED GRAPEFRUIT JUICE

In a cocktail shaker, muddle 1 sage leaf with the lemon juice and agave syrup and then add ice. Top with the moonshine and grapefruit juice. Shake and strain into a cocktail glass. Garnish with a sage leaf.

Whitney Vadeboncoeur, Dark Corner Distillery, Greenville, SC

THE BLACK BETTY

✳

1 PART FIREFLY BLACKBERRY MOONSHINE

1 PART KAHLÚA

Shake all with ice and strain into a shot glass.

BLACK ONYX
MARTINI

✳ ⟶

2 OZ. (60 ML) ONYX MOONSHINE

½ OZ. (15 ML) GINGER LIQUEUR

2 OZ. (60 ML) BLACK CURRANT JUICE

½ OZ. (15 ML) SIMPLE SYRUP

Shake all with ice and strain into a cocktail glass.

Onyx Spirits, East Hartford, CT

Al Capone

BLACKBEARD'S APPLE PIE

❋

2 OZ. (60 ML) MIDNIGHT MOON APPLE PIE
½ OZ. (15 ML) SPICED RUM

Shake all with ice and strain over fresh ice in an old-fashioned glass. Garnish with a lemon slice.

BLUE MICKEY

❋

3 OR 4 FRESH BLUEBERRIES
1 OZ. (30 ML) BLUEBERRY-INFUSED MOONSHINE
1 OZ. (30 ML) BOMBAY SAPPHIRE GIN
½ OZ. (15 ML) FRESH LIME JUICE
CLUB SODA TO TASTE

In a Collins glass, add the blueberries and fill with ice. In a cocktail shaker filled with ice, add the moonshine, gin, and lime juice. Shake and strain into the glass and fill the glass with club soda.

BLUE MOON

------------------------------ * ------------------------------>

2 OZ. (60 ML) DARK CORNER MOONSHINE
1 OZ. (30 ML) BLUE CURAÇAO
15 OZ. (445 ML) LEMONADE

Build over ice in an 18 oz. (.5 L) mason jar and stir. Garnish with a lemon wheel.

Whitney Vadeboncoeur, Dark Corner Distillery, Greenville, SC

BLUE SKY

------------------------------ * ------------------------------

1½ OZ. (45 ML) HIGH WEST SILVER WHISKEY
    OMG PURE RYE
1 OZ. (30 ML) FRESH LIME JUICE
1 BAR SPOON OF BLUEBERRY JAM
2-3 MINT SPRIGS
GINGER BEER TO TASTE

Combine the whiskey, lime juice, and blueberry jam in a cocktail shaker with ice and shake. Strain into an ice-filled Collins glass. Place mint in palm of hand and slap together with opposite hand. Stuff mint in glass and top with ginger beer. Garnish with more mint.

High West Distillery and Saloon, Park City, UT

BLUEBERRY BASILITO

✳

4 BASIL LEAVES

2 TSP. SUGAR

1½ OZ. (45 ML) FROZEN BLUEBERRIES

1 OZ. (30 ML) SPARKLING WATER

1½ OZ. (45 ML) MIDNIGHT MOON BLUEBERRY
   MOONSHINE

1 OZ. (30 ML) FRESH LIME JUICE

In a highball glass, add the basil, sugar, blueberries, and sparkling water and lightly muddle with a wooden muddler or a bar spoon. Fill with ice and add the moonshine and lime juice. Stir gently, garnish with a lime wheel, and serve with a straw.

BLUEBERRY CORN MUFFIN

✳

¼ CUP (30 G) FRESH BLUEBERRIES

¼ OZ. (7 ML) SIMPLE SYRUP

1 PINCH SALT

½ OZ. (15 ML) FRESH LEMON JUICE

2 OZ. (60 ML) GLEN THUNDER CORN WHISKEY

GINGER ALE TO TASTE

In a highball glass, muddle the berries, simple syrup, salt, and lemon juice. Add ice and the whiskey. Pour into a cocktail shaker and shake for 20 seconds. Pour back into the glass and top with ginger ale. Garnish with blueberries and a lemon wheel.

BLUEBERRY ROYALE

✳

2 OZ. (60 ML) MIDNIGHT MOON BLUEBERRY
    MOONSHINE
BRUT CHAMPAGNE TO TASTE

Build in a champagne flute. Garnish with a spear of fresh blueberries.

BOOTLEGGER'S PUMPKIN PIE

✳ ⟶

CINNAMON AND SUGAR
2 OZ. (60 ML) DARK CORNER MOONSHINE
    CORN WHISKEY
½ OZ. (15 ML) GINGER SYRUP
SPLASH OF ORANGE JUICE
1 TBSP. (18 G) PUMPKIN BUTTER
1 OZ. (30 ML) SPARKLING WINE

Rim a martini glass with a cinnamon-sugar mixture. In a cocktail shaker ¾ filled with ice, add the moonshine, ginger syrup, orange juice, and pumpkin butter. Shake and strain into the martini glass. Top with sparkling wine and garnish with an orange twist.

Whitney Vadeboncoeur, Dark Corner Distillery, Greenville, SC

BULLFROG

---✶---

1½ OZ. (45 ML) MOONSHINE

LEMONADE TO TASTE

Build over crushed ice in a Collins glass and garnish with a slice of lime.

CAIPIRINHA THUNDER

---✶--->

½ OF ONE LIME, CUT INTO QUARTERS

1 TSP. SUPERFINE SUGAR

2 OZ. (60 ML) GLEN THUNDER CORN WHISKEY

In a rocks glass, muddle the lime quarters and sugar until the lime is juiced. Add the whiskey and crushed ice to the glass and stir.

THE CARAMEL APPLE

❋

1 OZ. (30 ML) FIREFLY CARAMEL MOONSHINE
1 OZ. (30 ML) FIREFLY APPLE PIE MOONSHINE
APPLE CIDER TO TASTE

Build over ice in a mason jar and garnish with an apple slice.

THE CARAMEL BARREL

❋

1 PART FIREFLY CARAMEL MOONSHINE
1 PART BUFFALO TRACE BOURBON
2 MARASCHINO CHERRIES

Shake all with ice and strain into shot glasses. Add a single maraschino cherry to each shot.

THE CHARLES

❋

1 OZ. (30 ML) MOONSHINE

¾ OZ. (20 ML) PEACH BRANDY

1 OZ. (30 ML) FRESH LEMON JUICE

½ OZ. (15 ML) SIMPLE SYRUP

1 EGG WHITE

2 DASHES ORANGE BITTERS

Shake all but the bitters with ice and strain into a highball glass over fresh ice. Add the bitters and stir gently.

CAROLINA EGGNOG

❋

6 OZ. (180 ML) PREPARED EGGNOG

1½ OZ. (45 ML) PALMETTO MOONSHINE

CINNAMON TO TASTE

Heat the eggnog and moonshine in a mug or Irish coffee glass. Sprinkle with cinnamon and garnish with a cinnamon stick.

Palmetto Moonshine Distillery, Anderson, SC

CHERRY BOMB

*

2 OZ. (60 ML) PALMETTO MOONSHINE

½ OZ. (15 ML) AMARETTO

1 OZ. (30 ML) FRESH BLOOD ORANGE JUICE (YOU
CAN SUBSTITUTE WITH FRESH ORANGE JUICE)

½ OZ. (15 ML) FRESH LIME JUICE

½ OZ. (15 ML) MAPLE SYRUP

3 MARASCHINO CHERRIES

Line up three shot glasses, with sugared rims if desired. Combine all except the cherries in a cocktail shaker filled with ice and shake for 15–20 seconds. Strain into the glasses and garnish each glass with a single maraschino cherry.

Palmetto Moonshine Distillery, Anderson, SC

CHERRY BOUNCE

*

1 OZ. (30 ML) FIREFLY CHERRY MOONSHINE

1 OZ. (30 ML) FIREFLY SWEET TEA BOURBON

CLUB SODA TO TASTE

Build over ice in a mason jar and garnish with a maraschino cherry.

CHERRY MINT JULEP

4–6 MINT LEAVES

2 TSP. SUGAR

6 CHERRIES (PITTED, FROZEN)

2 TSP. WATER

½ OZ. (15 ML) MIDNIGHT MOON CHERRY
MOONSHINE

½ OZ. (15 ML) BOURBON

In a julep glass or other tall glass, muddle the mint leaves, sugar, cherries, and water. Fill the glass with crushed ice and add the moonshine and the bourbon. Top with more ice, garnish with a mint sprig, and serve with a straw.

CHOCOLATE CHERRY MOON

½ OZ. (15 ML) MIDNIGHT MOON CHERRY
MOONSHINE

¾ OZ. (20 ML) DARK CRÈME DE CACAO

4 DASHES OF BITTER TRUTH CHOCOLATE BITTERS

½ OZ. (15 ML) HALF & HALF

Shake all with ice and strain over fresh ice in a highball glass. Garnish with chocolate shavings.

Bootlegger Dutch Schultz

CHOCOLATE STRAWBERRIES

✳

2 OZ. (60 ML) MIDNIGHT MOON STRAWBERRY
    MOONSHINE
I OZ. (30 ML) WHITE CRÈME DE CACAO

Shake all with ice and strain into a martini glass. Garnish
with a chocolate-covered strawberry.

CITY SLICKER

✳

I OZ. (30 ML) PALMETTO MOONSHINE
I OZ. (30 ML) PATRÓN XO CAFE
½ OZ. (15 ML) GRAND MARNIER
I DOUBLE SHOT ESPRESSO

In a cocktail shaker filled with ice and a splash of water,
combine all ingredients and shake well. Pour all, including ice,
into a tall tumbler glass. The top should be nice and frothy.
Garnish with an orange slice.

Palmetto Moonshine Distillery, Anderson, SC

CLIFF HANGER

❋

1 SMALL PIECE FRESH GINGER

1 TSP. SIMPLE SYRUP

2 DASHES FEE BROTHERS RHUBARB BITTERS

¼ OZ. (7 ML) FRESH LEMON JUICE

1½ OZ. (45 ML) MOONSHINE

1½ OZ. (45 ML) PEAR NECTAR

½ OZ. (15 ML) GINGER LIQUEUR

In a cocktail shaker, muddle the ginger, simple syrup, bitters, and lemon juice. Fill the shaker with ice and add the moonshine, pear nectar, and ginger liqueur. Shake for 15–20 seconds and strain into a highball glass filled with fresh ice. Garnish with candied ginger and lime, if desired.

THE COOT MATTHEWS

* ❋ *

- 1 SLICE JALAPEÑO PEPPER
- 1 OZ. (30 ML) FRESH LIME JUICE
- 1 DASH FEE BROTHERS PEACH BITTERS
- 2 OZ. (60 ML) GLEN THUNDER CORN WHISKEY
- 1 OZ. (30 ML) APRICOT BRANDY
- SPLASH OF CLUB SODA

In a highball glass, muddle the pepper, lime juice, and bitters; then fill the glass with ice. Add the whiskey and apricot brandy and pour into a cocktail shaker and shake. Pour back into the glass and top with a splash of club soda. Garnish with a lime wedge and mint.

COPACETIC COCKTAIL

✴

2 OZ. (60 ML) MOONSHINE

½ OZ. (15 ML) ST-GERMAIN ELDERFLOWER LIQUEUR

¼ OZ. (7 ML) SAVANNA PEACH SCHNAPPS

½ OZ. (15 ML) BROWN SUGAR SIMPLE SYRUP

1 TBSP. (20 G) ORANGE MARMALADE

2 DASHES FEE BROTHERS RHUBARB BITTERS

Shake all with ice and strain into a highball glass over fresh ice.

CRANBERRY MOON

✴

1½ OZ. (45 ML) ONYX MOONSHINE

2 OZ. (60 ML) CRANBERRY JUICE

GINGER ALE TO TASTE

In a cocktail shaker filled with ice, combine the moonshine and cranberry juice and shake for 15–20 seconds. Strain into a highball glass filled with fresh ice. Top with ginger ale. Garnish with an orange twist.

Onyx Spirits, East Hartford, CT

CRANBERRY MOON SPARKLER

❋

- 1 oz. (30 ml) Dark Corner Moonshine Corn Whiskey
- 1 tsp. cranberry sauce
- ½ oz. (15 ml) fresh lemon juice
- pinch of ground ginger
- 2 oz. (60 ml) sparkling wine

In a cocktail shaker filled ¾ with ice, combine the moonshine, cranberry sauce, lemon juice, and ginger. Shake and strain into a champagne flute. Top with sparkling wine. Garnish with cranberries.

Whitney Vadeboncoeur, Dark Corner Distillery, Greenville, SC

CRANBERRY MOONSHINE COCKTAIL

❋

- 1½ oz. (45 ml) of Midnight Moon Cranberry Moonshine
- ½ oz. (15 ml) Grand Marnier
- chilled Aranciata Rossa San Pellegrino to taste

In a shaker filled with ice, combine the moonshine and Grand Marnier. Shake and strain into a martini glass and top with the San Pellegrino. Garnish with an orange twist.

CRASH AND BURN

✳

2 oz. (60 ml) Catdaddy Carolina Moonshine

1 oz. (30 ml) Bacardi Light Rum

1 oz. (30 ml) peach schnapps

1 oz. (30 ml) orange juice

1 oz. (30 ml) pineapple juice

Shake all with ice and strain into shot glasses.
Makes 7–8 shots.

CREAMED CORN

✳ ⟶

2 oz. (60 ml) Glen Thunder Corn Whiskey

2 dashes Fee Brothers Aztec
  Chocolate Bitters

cream soda to taste

Build over ice in a Collins glass or mason jar and stir. Serve
with a chocolate candy on the side.

DEVIL'S PUNCH

❋

3 FRESH BLACKBERRIES
2 OZ. (60 ML) PALMETTO MOONSHINE
½ OZ. (15 ML) FRESH LEMON JUICE
½ OZ. (15 ML) ORANGE JUICE
½ OZ. (15 ML) GRENADINE
½ OZ. (15 ML) SIMPLE SYRUP
CLUB SODA TO TASTE

In a cocktail shaker, muddle the blackberries; then fill the shaker with ice. Add the remaining ingredients, except the club soda, and shake for 15–20 seconds. Strain into a Collins glass filled with fresh ice and top with club soda.

Palmetto Moonshine Distillery, Anderson, SC

DIRTY WHITE DOG

❋ ⟶

2 OZ. (60 ML) DARK CORNER MOONSHINE
    CORN WHISKEY
1 OZ. (30 ML) OLIVE JUICE
DASH OF DRY VERMOUTH

Shake all with ice and strain into a cocktail glass. Garnish with olives.

Joe Fenten, Dark Corner Distillery, Greenville, SC

DOLLED-UP CAM

*

1 OZ. (30 ML) PEACH MOONSHINE

½ OZ. (15 ML) GRENADINE

GINGER ALE TO TASTE

Build over ice in a Collins glass and stir. Garnish with a cherry.

EASY DOES IT

*

½ OZ. (15 ML) BAILEYS IRISH CREAM

½ OZ. (15 ML) KAHLÚA

½ OZ. (15 ML) MOONSHINE

Layer in a shot glass in the order given.

FIRE AND ICE

※ ─────────→

½ OZ. (15 ML) APPLE PIE MOONSHINE
½ OZ. (15 ML) APPLE CIDER
½ OZ. (15 ML) OVERPROOF RUM

Build in a shot glass, floating the rum on top. Light the rum with a match and allow it to burn for no more than 5–10 seconds (or the glass will be too hot!). Extinguish with an inverted pint glass before drinking.

THE FIREFLY MOONRISE

※ ─────────

I PART FIREFLY PEACH MOONSHINE
I PART FIREFLY WHITE LIGHTNING MOONSHINE
ORANGE JUICE TO TASTE
SPLASH OF GRENADINE

Build over ice in a Collins glass, adding the moonshines and then filling the glass with orange juice. The grenadine will sink to the bottom to create a nice sunrise effect. Garnish with a slice of peach or an orange wheel.

FIREFLY PEACH PUNCH

1 oz. (30 ml) Firefly Peach Moonshine
1 oz. (30 ml) Firefly Caramel Moonshine
lemon-flavored sweet tea to taste

Build over ice in a mason jar and garnish with a lemon wedge.

FOREST FIRE

1 shot moonshine
2-3 dashes Tabasco sauce

Build in a shot glass.

FULL-MOON LEMONADE

✳

- 1 OZ. (30 ML) MOONSHINE
- 1 OZ. (30 ML) LIMONCELLO
- 1 OZ. (30 ML) LEMON JUICE
- 1 TSP. SUGAR

Shake all with ice and strain into a cocktail glass. Garnish with a lemon wheel.

GEORGIA SWAMP WATER

✳

- 2 OZ. (60 ML) MOONSHINE
- LEMONADE TO TASTE

Build over ice in a mason jar and stir. Garnish with a lemon wedge.

GIGGLE WATER

---- ✳ ----

1 OZ. (30 ML) MOONSHINE
1 OZ. (30 ML) LONDON GIN
½ OZ. (15 ML) TRIPLE SEC
TONIC WATER TO TASTE

Build over ice in a highball glass and top with tonic water. Garnish with a cherry and an orange wheel.

GIT'ER DUN

---- ✳ ---- →

1¼ OZ. (40 ML) PALMETTO MOONSHINE
¼ OZ. (7 ML) COINTREAU
1 OZ. (30 ML) SUNNYD
½ OZ. (15 ML) ROCKSTAR ORANGE ENERGY DRINK

In a cocktail shaker ¾ filled with ice, combine all. Shake vigorously for 15–20 seconds and strain into a highball glass filled with ice. Garnish with an orange wedge, if desired.

Palmetto Moonshine Distillery, Anderson, SC

GREEN GOBLIN

✳

1 OZ. (30 ML) MOONSHINE
½ OZ. (15 ML) BLUE CURAÇAO
2 OZ. (60 ML) ORANGE JUICE
2 OZ. (60 ML) PINEAPPLE JUICE

Shake all with ice and pour into a highball glass.

GREEN WITH ENVY

✳

2 CUCUMBER SLICES
1 TBSP. (15 ML) HONEY
½ OZ. (15 ML) FRESH LEMON JUICE
2 OZ. (60 ML) ONYX MOONSHINE
1 OZ. (30 ML) ST-GERMAIN ELDERFLOWER LIQUEUR
1 EGG WHITE

In a cocktail shaker, muddle the cucumber slices, honey, and lemon juice. Fill the shaker with ice and add the moonshine, St-Germain, and egg white and shake vigorously for 15–20 seconds. Pour into a highball glass.

Onyx Spirits, East Hartford, CT

HARD CORE

❋

1 OZ. (30 ML) OLE SMOKY APPLE PIE MOONSHINE
½ OZ. (15 ML) GRAND MARNIER
½ OZ. (15 ML) AMARETTO
COLA TO TASTE

Build over ice in a highball glass and stir. Garnish with an orange and cherry spear.

HARVEST MOON

❋

2 OZ. (60 ML) MOONSHINE
APPLE CIDER TO TASTE

Pour over ice in a highball glass and garnish with a slice of apple and a cinnamon stick.

THE HILLBILLY

SALT (OPTIONAL)

1 OZ. (30 ML) PALMETTO MOONSHINE

1 OZ. (30 ML) REPOSADO TEQUILA

1 TBSP. (15 ML) HONEY

JUICE OF ½ LIME

JUICE OF ½ GRAPEFRUIT

JUICE OF ½ BLOOD ORANGE

Salt the rim of a margarita glass, if desired. Shake all with ice and strain over fresh ice in the margarita glass. Garnish with a lime wheel.

Palmetto Moonshine Distillery, Anderson, SC

HONEYSUCKLE COSMO

1½ OZ. (45 ML) DARK CORNER HONEYSUCKLE SHINE

½ OZ. (15 ML) CRANBERRY JUICE

¼ OZ. (7 ML) TRIPLE SEC

¼ OZ. (7 ML) LIME JUICE

Shake all with ice and strain into a cocktail glass. Garnish with a lime wedge.

Raina Peck, Low Country-Backyard, Hilton Head Island, SC

JAILBIRD

---

2 OZ. (60 ML) FIREFLY STRAWBERRY MOONSHINE
GINGER ALE TO TASTE

Build over ice in a Collins glass. Garnish with a sliced strawberry.

JALAPEÑO OLD-FASHIONED

---

2 THIN JALAPEÑO SLICES
1 PINCH SALT
¼ OZ. (7 ML) ORANGE JUICE
¼ OZ. (7 ML) SIMPLE SYRUP
1 OZ. (30 ML) McKENZIE RYE WHISKEY
1 OZ. (30 ML) GLEN THUNDER CORN WHISKEY

In a shaker, muddle the jalapeño slices, salt, orange juice, and simple syrup. Fill the shaker ¾ full with ice and add the whiskies. Shake and strain into a highball glass over fresh ice. Garnish with an orange slice, if desired.

JAMAICAN ME SHINE

*

2 oz. (60 ml) Palmetto Moonshine

½ oz. (15 ml) fresh lemon juice

1 oz. (30 ml) simple syrup

2 oz. (60 ml) Jamaican-style ginger beer

In a cocktail shaker filled with ice, combine the moonshine, lemon juice, and simple syrup. Shake for 15–20 seconds and strain into a highball glass filled with fresh ice. Top with ginger beer.

Palmetto Moonshine Distillery, Anderson, SC

NOTE: Ginger beer comes in two styles—Bermuda and Jamaican. Jamaican has cayenne or another spice added to make it spicier.

JILL'S JUICE JOINT

✳

SPLASH OF GRENADINE

1 OZ. (30 ML) APPLE PIE MOONSHINE

1 OZ. (30 ML) PEACH MOONSHINE

½ OZ. PEACH SCHNAPPS

1 OZ. (30 ML) PEAR NECTAR

CLUB SODA TO TASTE

SPLASH OF ORANGE JUICE

Add a splash of grenadine to the bottom of a Collins glass and fill the glass with ice. In a cocktail shaker filled with ice, add the apple pie moonshine, peach moonshine, peach schnapps, and pear nectar. Shake for 15–20 seconds and strain slowly into the Collins glass. Almost fill the glass with club soda and float a splash of orange juice on top. Garnish with an orange wheel.

JUNE BUG

---✦--->

½ OZ. (15 ML) MOONSHINE
½ OZ. (15 ML) GREEN CRÈME DE MENTHE
SPLASH OF FRESH LEMON JUICE

Shake all with ice and strain into a cocktail glass. Garnish with a mint sprig and a lemon wheel.

JUNIOR'S
CHERRY BOURBON

---✦---

2 OZ. (60 ML) MIDNIGHT MOON CHERRY
   MOONSHINE
1 OZ. (30 ML) BOURBON
SPLASH OF GINGER ALE

Pour the moonshine and bourbon into a shaker and shake over ice. Strain into a glass filled with fresh ice and top with a splash of ginger ale.

Machine Gun Kelly

KELLY'S CAPER

* *

½ OZ. (15 ML) SIMPLE SYRUP (OR HONEY)

8 MINT LEAVES

2 OZ. (60 ML) MOONSHINE

1 OZ. (30 ML) PINEAPPLE JUICE

½ OZ. (15 ML) FRESH LIME JUICE

In a cocktail shaker, add the simple syrup (or honey) and mint and muddle. Fill the shaker with ice and add the moonshine, pineapple juice, and lime juice. Shake for 15–20 seconds and pour into a highball glass. Garnish with an orange wheel.

KING'S CHOCOLATE NUT

* *

1 PART KINGS COUNTY CHOCOLATE WHISKEY
    (CHOCOLATE-INFUSED MOONSHINE)

1 PART KAHLÚA

1 PART FRANGELICO

Shake all with ice and strain into a shot glass.

KING'S WHITE CHOCOLATE

2 OZ. (60 ML) KINGS COUNTY CHOCOLATE WHISKEY
(CHOCOLATE-INFUSED MOONSHINE)
1 OZ. (30 ML) KAHLÚA
2 OZ. (60 ML) MILK

Shake all with ice and pour into a highball glass. Garnish with chocolate shavings or a chocolate-dipped straw.

LEMON LIGHTNING

1 OZ. (30 ML) OLE SMOKY TENNESSEE MOONSHINE
½ OZ. (15 ML) FRESH LEMON JUICE

Store the moonshine in the freezer for at least 8 hours. Combine the moonshine with the lemon juice in a shot glass, allowing the lemon juice to be chilled by the moonshine.

LOVER'S MOON

✳

2 OZ. (60 ML) MOONSHINE
JUICE OF ½ LEMON
1 TSP. GRENADINE
LEMON-LIME SODA TO TASTE

For two lovebirds, build over ice in a mason jar and garnish with fresh strawberries, orange slices, and two straws.

LOW-HANGING FRUIT

✳

1 OZ. (30 ML) BLACKBERRY-INFUSED MOONSHINE
1 OZ. (30 ML) GREY GOOSE LA POIRE PEAR VODKA
½ OZ. (15 ML) CHAMBORD

Shake all with ice and strain into a cocktail glass. Garnish with fresh blackberries.

MOON AND STARS WATERMELON MARTINI

*

3 ONE-INCH CUBES OF WATERMELON

PINCH COARSE KOSHER SALT

1½ OZ. (45 ML) JUNIOR JOHNSON'S MIDNIGHT MOON

¾ OZ. (20 ML) FRESH LIME JUICE

¾ OZ. (20 ML) SIMPLE SYRUP

2 DASHES MEMPHIS BARBECUE BITTERS

Muddle the watermelon in a cocktail shaker and add the salt. Fill the shaker ¾ full with ice and add the moonshine, lime juice, simple syrup, and bitters. Shake vigorously for 15–20 seconds and strain into a cocktail glass. Garnish with a thinly sliced watermelon wedge.

MOON CAFÉ

*

CINNAMON AND SUGAR

1½ OZ. (45 ML) DARK CORNER MOONSHINE
   CORN WHISKEY

1 OZ. (30 ML) COFFEE LIQUEUR

1 SHOT OF ESPRESSO

Rim a cocktail glass with a cinnamon-sugar mixture. In a shaker filled with ice, add the whiskey, coffee liqueur, and shot of espresso. Shake until frothy and strain into the cocktail glass.

Whitney Vadeboncoeur, Dark Corner Distillery, Greenville, SC

MOONLIGHT

*

1½ OZ. (45 ML) MOONSHINE

LIGHT BEER TO TASTE

2 DASHES TABASCO SAUCE

Add the moonshine to a highball glass and fill with beer. Add Tabasco sauce and stir gently.

MOON TANG

*

2 OZ. (60 ML) PALMETTO MOONSHINE

1 OZ. (30 ML) DEKUYPER WATERMELON PUCKER

1 OZ. (30 ML) SIMPLE SYRUP

TANG TO TASTE

In a cocktail shaker filled with ice, combine the moonshine, Watermelon Pucker, and simple syrup and shake for 15–20 seconds. Strain into a Collins glass or tumbler filled with fresh, crushed ice. Top with Tang. Garnish with a thinly sliced watermelon wedge.

Palmetto Moonshine Distillery, Anderson, SC

MOONSHINE BAY BREEZE

*

1½ OZ. (45 ML) MOONSHINE

2 OZ. (60 ML) PINEAPPLE JUICE

2 OZ. (60 ML) CRANBERRY JUICE

Shake all with ice and pour into a highball glass. Garnish with a pineapple, orange, and cherry spear.

MOONSHINE DAIQUIRI

*

2 OZ. (60 ML) MOONSHINE

1 OZ. (30 ML) FRESH LIME JUICE

2 TSP. SUPERFINE SUGAR

CLUB SODA TO TASTE

Shake all but the club soda with ice and strain into a Collins glass filled with fresh ice. Top with club soda and garnish with a lime wheel.

MOONSHINE MARGARITA

❋

¾ OZ. (20 ML) ROCK TOWN ARKANSAS LIGHTNING
1½ OZ. (45 ML) ROCK TOWN PEACH LIGHTNING
2 OZ. (60 ML) LIME JUICE

Combine all in a cocktail shaker with ice, shake until cold, and then pour into a margarita glass. Garnish with a lime wedge.

Rock Town Distillery, Little Rock, AR

MOONSHINE MARY

❋

1 OZ. (30 ML) MOONSHINE
½ OZ. (15 ML) LEMON JUICE
4 OZ. (120 ML) TOMATO JUICE
WORCESTERSHIRE SAUCE TO TASTE
GRATED HORSERADISH TO TASTE
KOSHER SALT TO TASTE
FINELY GROUND BLACK PEPPER TO TASTE

Combine all with ice in a cocktail shaker and shake for 15–20 seconds. Pour into a Collins glass and garnish with a celery stalk and whatever other trimmings you enjoy with a traditional Bloody Mary.

MOONSHINE MULE

＊

2 OZ. (60 ML) MOONSHINE
1 TSP. SIMPLE SYRUP
JUICE OF ½ OF A LIME
BERMUDA-STYLE GINGER BEER

Combine the moonshine, simple syrup, and lime juice in a highball glass with ice and stir. Top with ginger beer and garnish with a lime wedge or lime wheel.

MOONSHINE SANGRIA

＊

8 OZ. (240 ML) APPLE PIE MOONSHINE
4 OZ. (120 ML) MOONSHINE
1 BOTTLE DRY RED WINE
2 OZ. (60 ML) GRAND MARNIER
16 OZ. (470 ML) ORANGE JUICE
1 ORANGE, SLICED INTO ROUNDS
1 LEMON, SLICED INTO ROUNDS
1 LIME, SLICED INTO ROUNDS
1 APPLE, SLICED INTO WEDGES

Combine everything in a glass pitcher and refrigerate overnight.

MOONTOONI

2½ OZ. (75 ML) MOONSHINE

½ OZ. (15 ML) DRY VERMOUTH

2 DASHES ANGOSTURA BITTERS

Shake or stir all with ice and strain into a cocktail glass.

MOUNTAIN HIGHBALL

---

2 OZ. (60 ML) MOONSHINE

MOUNTAIN DEW TO TASTE

Build over ice in a Collins glass and stir. Garnish with a maraschino cherry.

OLD-FASHIONED APPLE PIE

✳

1 ORANGE SLICE
1½ OZ. (45 ML) MIDNIGHT MOON APPLE PIE MOONSHINE
1½ OZ. (45 ML) RYE WHISKY
5 DASHES BITTERS

Muddle the orange slice in a glass. Fill the glass with ice and add all other ingredients. Stir gently.

OLE SMOKY
BLACKBERRY TEA

✳

1 GALLON (3.75 L) OF FRESHLY BREWED BLACK TEA
    (SEE INSTRUCTIONS)
2 JARS OF OLE SMOKY BLACKBERRY
    MOONSHINE
1 CUP (200 G) SUGAR
1 LEMON SLICED INTO THIN ROUNDS

Tie together 16 tea bags to a single, long string. Add 1 gallon of water (3.75 L) to a 2-gallon (7.5-L) clear glass jug. Add the tea bags to the jug allowing the string to hang outside, and cover the top with a cap or with foil. Place the jug in the sun and allow the tea to brew for up to an hour. Remove the tea bags and add the moonshine, sugar, and lemon slices.

OLE SMOKY FRONT PORCH TEA

* →

2 OZ. (60 ML) OLE SMOKY PEACH MOONSHINE

1 PART FRESHLY BREWED SWEET TEA

1 PART LEMONADE

In a Collins glass or mason jar, add the moonshine. Fill the jar with equal parts tea and lemonade.

ORANGE SLIDER

*

1 OZ. (30 ML) PALMETTO MOONSHINE

1 OZ. (30 ML) COINTREAU

1 OZ. (30 ML) PIÑA COLADA MIX

ORANGE JUICE TO TASTE

In a cocktail shaker filled with ice, combine the moonshine, Cointreau, and piña colada mix and shake for 15–20 seconds. Strain into a highball glass filled with fresh ice. Top with orange juice. Garnish with an orange wheel.

Palmetto Moonshine Distillery, Anderson, SC

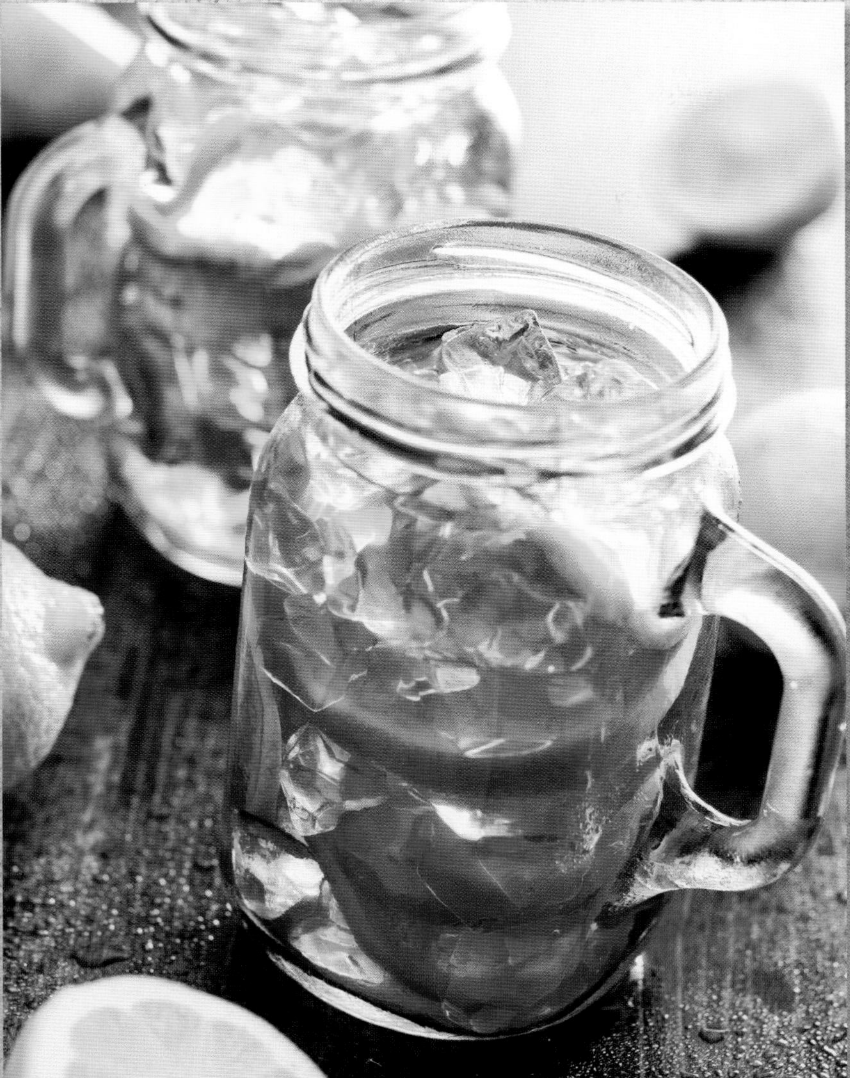

OSSIFIED EILEEN

❋

1 OZ. (30 ML) MOONSHINE

1 OZ. (30 ML) CHAMBORD

OAK-FINISHED CHARDONNAY TO TASTE

Build over ice in a large tumbler or water glass. Garnish with a fresh raspberry, orange, and cherry spear.

PINK LEMONADE

❋ ⟶

2 OZ. (60 ML) MOONSHINE

½ OZ. (15 ML) COINTREAU

PINK LEMONADE TO TASTE

Build over ice in a Collins glass and stir. Garnish with a lemon wheel.

POMEGRANATE SPARKLE AND SHINE

❋

1 TBSP. (10 G) POMEGRANATE SEEDS

½ OZ. (15 ML) DARK CORNER MOONSHINE CORN
   WHISKEY

½ OZ. (15 ML) FRESH LEMON JUICE

¼ OZ. (7ML) GRENADINE

1 OZ. (30 ML) SPARKLING WINE

Place the of pomegranate seeds in the bottom of a champagne flute. In a cocktail shaker filled with ice, combine the moonshine with the lemon juice and grenadine. Shake and strain slowly into the flute so that the seeds stay at the bottom. (The seeds will slowly rise up as the beverage is consumed.) Top with sparkling wine and garnish with a lemon twist.

Whitney Vadeboncoeur, Dark Corner Distillery, Greenville, SC

PONDEROSA

❋

2 OZ. (60 ML) MOONSHINE

ORANGE SODA TO TASTE

Build over ice in a Collins glass or mason jar. Garnish with an orange slice.

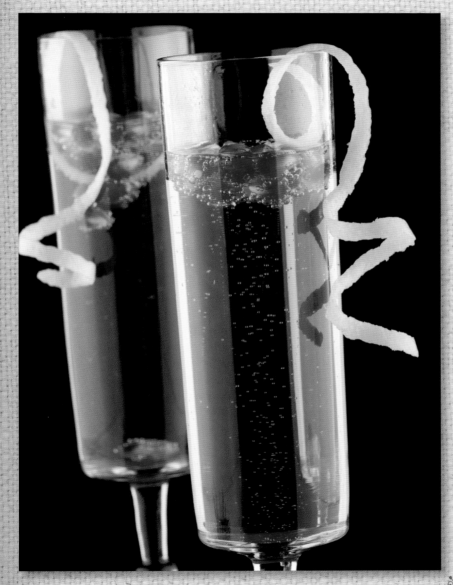

RAT-A-TAT COBBLER

— ✳ —

8 FRESH RASPBERRIES

1 ORANGE WEDGE

½ OZ. (15 ML) DR. MCGILLICUDDY'S RAW
VANILLA SCHNAPPS

½ OZ. (15 ML) CHAMBORD

2 OZ. (60 ML) MOONSHINE

In a cocktail shaker, add the raspberries, orange, vanilla schnapps, and Chambord and muddle. Fill the shaker with ice and add the moonshine. Shake for 15–20 seconds and strain into a highball glass filled with fresh ice. Garnish with a fresh raspberry and an orange wheel.

THE RATTLER

※

¾ OZ. (20 ML) FRESH LIME JUICE

6–10 MINT LEAVES

1 SLICE CUCUMBER

2 THIN SLICES FUJI APPLE

½ OZ. (15 ML) PALMETTO MOONSHINE

1 OZ. (30 ML) SIMPLE SYRUP

In a cocktail shaker, muddle the lime juice, mint, cucumber, and apple. Add the moonshine and simple syrup and fill the shaker with ice. Shake for 15–20 seconds and strain into an old-fashioned glass filled with fresh ice. Garnish with a cucumber wheel and a mint sprig.

Palmetto Moonshine Distillery, Anderson, SC

THE REBEL

❋

1¼ oz. (40 ml) Palmetto Moonshine

½ oz. (15 ml) fresh lemon juice

½ oz. (15 ml) pineapple juice

1 tsp. simple syrup

Mountain Dew to taste

Shake the moonshine, lemon juice, pineapple juice, and simple syrup in a cocktail shaker with ice for 15–20 seconds. Strain into a Collins glass over fresh ice and top with Mountain Dew.

Palmetto Moonshine Distillery, Anderson, SC

RED PEARL

*

- 1–3 JALAPEÑO SLICES
- 3 THAI BASIL LEAVES
- 4 CUBES OF PEELED KIWI
- 1½ OZ. (45 ML) GLEN THUNDER CORN WHISKEY
- ¼ OZ. (7 ML) CITRUS SOUR (SEE INSTRUCTIONS)
- ¼ OZ. (7 ML) SIMPLE SYRUP

In a shaker, muddle the jalapeño (use more or less to achieve the desired spiciness), Thai basil leaves, and kiwi cubes. Add the whiskey, citrus sour, and simple syrup and fill ¾ full with ice. Shake and pour into a highball glass.

TO MAKE CITRUS SOUR: Combine 1 part each of lime juice, lemon juice, orange juice, and simple syrup.

RED, WHITE-LIGHTNING, AND BLUE

❋

3 OR 4 FRESH BLUEBERRIES
½ OZ. (15 ML) MOONSHINE
½ OZ. (15 ML) CRANBERRY JUICE
LEMON-LIME SODA TO TASTE

Add the blueberries to the bottom of a cocktail glass. In a cocktail shaker filled with ice, combine the moonshine and cranberry juice and shake for 15–20 seconds. Strain into the cocktail glass and top with lemon-lime soda.

RISE-AND-'SHINE BELLINI

❋

1 OZ. (30 ML) OLE SMOKY PEACH MOONSHINE
½ OZ. (15 ML) PEACH PUREE (OR PEACH NECTAR)
SPARKLING WINE TO TASTE

In a champagne flute, add the moonshine and the peach puree. Fill with sparkling wine.

RUN FOR THE MOON

＊

1½ oz. (45 ml) moonshine
½ oz. (15 ml) fresh lemon juice
½ oz. (15 ml) Dr. McGillicuddy's Raw
  Vanilla Schnapps
root beer to taste

Shake all but the root beer with ice and strain into a Collins glass filled with fresh ice. Fill with root beer and garnish with a lemon wheel.

SAKE STORM

＊

1 oz. (30 ml) Glen Thunder Corn Whiskey
2 oz. (60 ml) sake
¼ oz. (7 ml) Galliano

Combine all in a cocktail shaker with ice. Shake and strain into a chilled martini glass. Garnish with a lemon twist.

SHOTGUN WEDDING

✳

2 OZ. (60 ML) MOONSHINE

½ OZ. (15 ML) COINTREAU

¼ OZ. (7 ML) AMARETTO

¼ OZ. (7 ML) GRENADINE

SPLASH OF PINEAPPLE JUICE

Shake all with ice and strain into a cocktail glass.

SIMPLE 'SHINE
AND SODA

✳ ⟶

2 OZ. (60 ML) MOONSHINE

LEMON-LIME SODA

Build over ice in a Collins glass or a mason jar and garnish with a lemon or lime wedge.

SOUTHERN DELIGHT

✳

1 OZ. (30 ML) PALMETTO MOONSHINE

2 OZ. (60 ML) DEKUYPER BUTTERSHOTS

1 TBSP. (15 ML) CHOCOLATE SYRUP

MILK TO TASTE

In a cocktail shaker filled with ice, combine the moonshine, Buttershots, and chocolate syrup and shake for 15–20 seconds. Strain into a highball glass filled with fresh ice. Top with milk. Garnish with chocolate shavings and whipped cream.

Palmetto Moonshine Distillery, Anderson, SC

SOUTHERN SUNRISE

✳

1 OZ. (30 ML) GLEN THUNDER WHISKEY

6 OZ. (180 ML) FRESH-SQUEEZED ORANGE JUICE

½ OZ. (15 ML) GRENADINE

Build over ice in a Collins glass; do not stir. Garnish with a cherry and an orange wheel.

SPLITDOG FITZ

1½ oz. (45 ml) Midnight Moon Strawberry
½ oz. (15 ml) simple syrup
¾ oz. (20 ml) fresh lemon juice
5 dashes Kansas City Smoked Bitters
craft wheat beer to taste

In a small shaker half filled with ice, add the moonshine, simple syrup, lemon juice, and bitters. Shake for 15–20 seconds. Fill a highball glass with ice and strain the shaker into the glass. Top with a good craft wheat beer. Garnish with a mint sprig and a strawberry.

STONE-COLD SOUR

1½ oz. (45 ml) Glen Thunder Corn Whiskey
¾ oz. (20 ml) fresh lemon juice
¾ oz. (20 ml) orange juice
½ oz. (15 ml) simple syrup

Shake all with ice and strain into a cocktail glass. Garnish with a cherry and an orange wheel.

STRAIGHT SHOOTER

❋

1 LEMON WEDGE

GRANULATED SUGAR

1½ OZ. (45 ML) PALMETTO MOONSHINE

Rub the rim of a shot glass with the lemon wedge and dip into a saucer of granulated sugar to rim the glass. Fill the glass with the moonshine. Knock back the shot and bite the lemon wedge.

Palmetto Moonshine Distillery, Anderson, SC

STRAWBERRY ROOT BEER

❋

2 OZ. (60 ML) FIREFLY STRAWBERRY MOONSHINE

ROOT BEER TO TASTE

Build over ice in a Collins glass and stir. Garnish with a cherry.

SUMMER BREEZE

—— ✳ ——

1 TSP. SUGAR (PREFERABLY SUGAR IN THE RAW)

4 MINT LEAVES

½ OF A LIME CUT INTO 4 CUBES

5 BLUEBERRIES

2 STRAWBERRIES, SLICED

2 OZ. (60 ML) DARK CORNER MOONSHINE
CORN WHISKEY

In a highball glass, combine the sugar, mint leaves, lime, blueberries, and strawberries and muddle with a wooden muddler or a bar spoon. Top with ice, add the moonshine, and stir.

Paolo Varvaro, The Cigar Boxx, Greenville, SC

SUPERFLY

—— ✳ ——

1 OZ. (30 ML) HIGH WEST SILVER WHISKEY
OMG PURE RYE

¾ OZ. (20 ML) GREEN CHARTREUSE

¾ OZ. (20 ML) FRESH LIME JUICE

2 OZ. (60 ML) GINGER BEER

Combine the whiskey, green Chartreuse, and lime juice in a cocktail shaker with ice and shake. Strain into an ice-filled Collins glass and top with the ginger beer. Garnish with a lime wheel.

High West Distillery and Saloon, Park City, UT

TANGERINE GINGER CAIPIRINHA

---

1 TSP. CHOPPED FRESH GINGER

½ TANGERINE, CUT INTO QUARTERS

1 TSP. SUGAR

2 OZ. (60 ML) GLEN THUNDER CORN WHISKEY

In a highball glass, muddle the chopped ginger, tangerine pieces, and sugar. Add the whiskey and stir. Fill with crushed ice or a single, large ice cube.

TEA TO SHINING TEA

---

2 OZ. (60 ML) ONYX MOONSHINE

SPLASH OF FRESH LEMON JUICE

SWEETENED ICED TEA TO TASTE

Build over ice in a tall glass and stir.

Onyx Spirits, East Hartford, CT.

THIRSTY IN L.A.

❋

1 oz. (30 ml) lemongrass-infused Martini & Rossi Bianco vermouth (see instructions)

¾ oz. (20 ml) High West Silver Whiskey OMG Pure Rye

¼ oz. (7 ml) Aperol

¼ oz. (7 ml) Nonino Grappa

3 dashes Peychaud's Bitters

sparkling white wine to taste

Place all except the sparkling white wine into a cocktail shaker with ice and stir. Strain into a chilled coupe glass and top with a splash of sparkling white wine. Garnish with a lemon twist.

High West Distillery and Saloon, Park City, UT

TO MAKE LEMONGRASS-INFUSED BIANCO VERMOUTH:

Take a small bunch of fresh lemongrass stalks and remove and discard the tops. Slice open the bottoms and add them to a 1-liter bottle of Martini & Rossi Bianco vermouth. Let the bottle sit in the refrigerator for at least 24 hours.

THUNDERHOUND

❖

2 OZ. (60 ML) GLEN THUNDER CORN WHISKEY
JUICE OF ½ A GRAPEFRUIT
¼ OZ. (7 ML) SIMPLE SYRUP

Shake all with ice and strain into a highball glass over fresh ice.

TRASH CAN PUNCH

✳

2 JARS OLE SMOKY MOONSHINE

3-4 GALLONS (11-15 L) OF DRINK MIX
(PICK YOUR FAVORITE FLAVOR)

6 ORANGES, SLICED THIN

6 APPLES, SLICED THIN

3 LEMONS, SLICED THIN

3 LIMES, SLICED THIN

Combine all in a large (5-gallon/20-liter) container. Pour in a bag of ice to chill it down or serve the ice on the side. Traditionally, this was made in a small trash can with a plastic garbage bag lining the can to keep the punch clean and to prevent leaks. A large beverage cooler will work just as well, but will not have the visual appeal.

WATERMELON COOLER

❋

4 CUBES OF FRESH, RIPE WATERMELON

½ OZ. (15 ML) FRESH LEMON JUICE

1½ OZ. (45 ML) MOONSHINE

4 OZ. (120 ML) LEMONADE

SPLASH OF LEMON-LIME SODA

In a cocktail shaker, add the watermelon and lemon juice and muddle. Fill the shaker with ice and add the moonshine. Shake for 15–20 seconds and strain into a Collins glass filled with fresh ice. Top with lemonade and a splash of lemon-lime soda. Garnish with a lemon wheel.

WHITE TRASH LEMONADE

*

4 OZ. (120 ML) OF CLOVER HONEY

8 OZ. (240 ML) HOT WATER

4 OZ. (120 ML) FRESH LEMON JUICE

⅛ TSP. SALT

8 OZ. (240 ML) PALMETTO MOONSHINE

1 LEMON, SLICED

4 OZ. (120 ML) COLD WATER

In a pitcher, mix the honey and hot water and stir to dissolve. Allow to cool. Add the lemon juice, salt, moonshine, and lemon slices. Refrigerate for several hours or overnight. Add cold water. Fill the pitcher with ice before serving. Pour into tall tumblers or water glasses filled with ice. Garnish with fresh mint, if desired.

Palmetto Moonshine Distillery, Anderson, SC

WHITE WHISKEY OLD-FASHIONED COCKTAIL

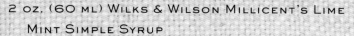

- 2 oz. (60 ml) Wilks & Wilson Millicent's Lime Mint Simple Syrup
- 4 drops Basement Bitters from Tuthilltown Spirits
- 2 home-cured cherries (see below)
- 4 oz. (120 ml) Hudson New York Corn Whiskey
- splash of Perrier Sparkling Natural Mineral Water (lemon essence)
- 2 oz. (60 ml) Carpano Antica Formula Sweet Vermouth

Fill a cocktail shaker ¾ with ice. Add the simple syrup, bitters, and cherries and muddle with a wooden muddler or with a bar spoon. Add 2 oz. (60 ml) of the whiskey and a splash of sparkling water and stir. Add the vermouth and the remaining 2 oz. (60 ml) of the whiskey and stir again. Strain into an old-fashioned glass or a highball glass.

Recipe courtesy of Warren Bobrow and Tuthilltown Spirits, Gardiner, NY

To make home-cured cherries, pour the bourbon over fresh bing cherries and let them steep for 2–3 weeks in a covered container in the refrigerator.

ZING CHERRY

✳

2 OZ. (60 ML) FIREFLY CHERRY MOONSHINE
DR PEPPER TO TASTE

Build over ice in a mason jar and garnish with a maraschino cherry.

BARTENDING TOOLS

———————— ✳ ————————

BAR MATS—Also known as spill stops, these are great for pouring shots on. The mat traps the spillage and keeps the bar neat. Don't forget to empty the mats and wash them.

BAR RAGS—You should always keep at least two bar rags handy to wipe up the inevitable spills and keep the bar clean.

BAR SPOON—A bar spoon is simply a small spoon with a very long handle. It has many uses behind the bar. It can be used for stirring cocktails, of course, but you can also pour a liqueur over the back of the spoon when layering it on top of another liqueur. You can also use it to scrape the bottom of a blender.

BLENDER—What bar would be complete without a blender for those fancy frozen drinks? A heavy-duty, multispeed blender is a good choice.

BOSTON SHAKER—This is a less elegant, but easier, cheaper, and more reliable alternative to the martini shaker. It consists of a metal cup and a pint glass. Ice and liquids are placed in the cup and the glass is placed tightly over the cup, forming a seal. You then shake and serve. Since a Boston shaker does not have a strainer built in, you will need a separate strainer if the drink needs to be strained.

GARNISH TRAY—A nice, neat, covered tray to keep your lemon slices, lime wedges, orange wheels, and cherries on is good to have.

ICE SCOOP—All commercial establishments require the use of a separate scoop for use with ice. There are good reasons for this, so even if you're at home, it's wise to use an ice scoop. First, if you use a glass to scoop the ice you run the risk of chipping the glass—imagine trying to find a glass chip in an ice bin! Second, your hands, used glassware, and any other potentially dirty object should never

*Bar tools (from left): bar spoon, strainer, tongs, jigger,
citrus zester with melon baller, muddler, shaker.*

come in contact with the ice. Ice is legally considered a food, so all the handling
procedures apply.

JIGGER—A jigger is simply a measuring device. It consists of two metal cups
welded bottom to bottom. One holds 1.5 ounces (45 ml) and the other is
1 ounce (30 ml). Some fancier jiggers have a handle.

KNIFE—A good, sharp knife is essential for cutting fruit for garnish wedges
or slices.

LIQUOR POURS—A liquor pour, also called a spout, is used to control the flow
of liquor from the bottle. This helps to prevent spilling and splashing and also
controls under- or overpouring. With a little practice, a bartender can accurately
pour an ounce by using a liquor pour and counting. Most pours flow at 1 ounce
per second. Another kind of liquor pour is a "measured pour" where the pour has
a built-in measurement and stops after that amount. For an example of this, see
the Sure Shot Pourers by Precision Pours.

Glass types (from left): old-fashioned, cocktail (martini), highball, flute, hurricane, wine, welled margarita, brandy snifter, and double shot.

SHAKER—Also called a "cocktail shaker" or "martini shaker," this is the classic shaker. A shaker has three parts: the cup, the top, and the cap. Place ice and then the liquids into the cup, put the top and the cap tightly onto the cup, and shake (away from the customer!). To serve, remove the cap and the top works as a strainer.

STRAINER—A strainer fits over the top of a Boston shaker, or any other glass, and is used to strain the ice from a drink after it's been stirred or shaken.

WINE OPENER—Any bar that serves wine should have a wine opener. Anything will do, from a simple corkscrew, to a fancy "estate" wine opener that mounts on the edge of the bar. The most popular is the "waiter's corkscrew," which is small, easy to use, and folds up so it can be kept in a pocket.

DRINK STYLES

---✴---

APERITIF—An alcoholic drink taken before a meal or any of several wines or bitters.

BUCK—A drink made with an ounce of liquor with lemon juice and ginger ale, and topped with a twist of lemon.

CHASER—A beverage you drink after doing a shot of whiskey or other spirit instead of being combined with a spirit in the glass. The original chaser was the boilermaker, which was a shot and a beer.

COBBLER—A tall summer-style drink that consists of ice, wine or liqueur, and a variety of fruit slices, cherries, berries, and so forth.

COLLINS—Tall, cool, punch-like drinks. Any basic liquor with lime or lemon juice over ice cubes in a frosted glass with sugar and soda water added. (Tom Collins is made with gin, John with whiskey, and Joe with scotch.)

COOLER—A low-alcohol drink consisting of either white or red wine mixed with either lemon-lime soda, ginger ale, club soda, or a citrus juice.

DRY—A term applied to any form of wine or liqueur to denote a lack of sweetness.

FIX—A sour drink, usually made with pineapple juice and crushed ice.

FIZZ—A drink made from liquor, citrus juices, and sugar, shaken with ice and strained into a highball glass. Soda "fizz" water is then added. Any carbonated beverage, even champagne, may be used to make the drink fizz.

FLIP—An eggnog and fizz combination. Made with liquor, egg, sugar, and shaved ice, shaken well, and sprinkled with nutmeg.

FRAPPÉ—A drink made by packing a glass with crushed ice and pouring liqueur over it.

HIGHBALL—Any liquor served with ice and soda or other carbonated beverages.

(From left:) Collins, fizz, highball.

JULEP—A liquor drink (traditionally bourbon) and fresh mint leaves (muddled, crushed, or whole), served in a frosted glass with shaved ice and a mint garnish.

LOWBALL—A short drink consisting of spirits served with ice alone, or with water or soda in a short glass. Also known as an on-the-rocks or old-fashioned.

MIST—A glass packed with crushed ice to which spirits are added, usually straight.

NEAT—A straight shot of any spirit taken in a single gulp, usually without any accompaniment, also called a shooter.

PICK-ME-UP—Any concoction designed to allay the effects of overindulgence in alcoholic beverages.

POUSSE-CAFÉ—A sweet, multilayered after-dinner drink. Success in making one depends upon keeping each layer separate and distinct from the others. The secret is knowing the relative heaviness of the various liquids that make up the pousse-café and adding them from heaviest to lightest.

RICKEY—A drink that is a cross between a Collins and a sour, but with no sugar. It consists of lime or lemon juice, club soda, and alcohol.

(From left:) Julep, shooter, toddy.

SANGAREE—A drink made with whiskey, gin, rum, or brandy, with port wine, wine, ale porter, or stout floated on top, with a sprinkle of nutmeg.

SHOOTER—A straight shot of spirits taken neat or with a mixture of spirits and other ingredients chilled and strained into a shot glass.

SLING—A drink made like a sangaree, with the addition of lemon juice and a twist of lemon peel. Served in an old-fashioned glass.

SMASH—A small julep, served in an old-fashioned glass, made with muddled sugar; ice cubes; whiskey, gin, rum, or brandy; and soda water.

SOUR—Any drink made with lemon juice, ice, sugar, and any basic liquor.

SWIZZLE—Originally a tall rum cooler filled with cracked ice that was "swizzled" with a long stirring rod or spoon rotated rapidly between the palms of the hands to produce frost on the glass.

TODDY—Originally a hot drink made with spirits, sugar, spices such as cinnamon or cloves, and a lemon peel mixed with hot water and served in a tall glass. Toddys can also be cold.

BARTENDING TECHNIQUES

———————— ✳ ————————

Throughout the recipes in this book, the following techniques are used to create the drinks. In the instructions, they are given as a shorthand notation for how to mix the drinks. Below is a more complete explanation of each of these.

BUILD IN A HEATPROOF CUP OR MUG—Combine the ingredients in a heatproof container such as a coffee mug or Irish coffee cup and then add the ingredients in the order listed. This is typically called for with hot drinks such as an Irish coffee.

BUILD IN THE GLASS WITH NO ICE—Add the ingredients to the glass without ice. This is typically called for when the ingredients are already cold and should not be diluted with ice. For example, most champagne-based or beer-based drinks are created this way.

BUILD OVER ICE AND STIR—Fill the glass with ice and add the ingredients. Then stir the drink with a stir stick or a bar spoon. You can also simply place the stirrer or straw into the drink and let the customer stir it.

BUILD OVER ICE—Fill the glass with ice and add the ingredients, allowing them to mix naturally. This is the method used to create the "sunrise" effect in a tequila sunrise.

COMBINE ALL INGREDIENTS IN A BLENDER WITH ICE. BLEND UNTIL SMOOTH—Add ice to the blender and then add all the ingredients. Blend everything until smooth. This is the method commonly used for most frozen drinks.

COMBINE ALL INGREDIENTS IN A BLENDER. BLEND UNTIL SMOOTH—Place all

the ingredients in the blender without adding any ice. Blend everything until smooth. This is the method commonly used for drinks made with ice cream.

LAYER IN A SHOT GLASS—Layer each of the ingredients in a shot glass or a pousse-café glass. Layering is a technique that requires a little bit of practice. The trick is to place a bar spoon upside down against the inner rim of the glass above the first ingredient. Then gently pour the next ingredient over the back of the spoon. This helps prevent the liquor from going into the glass too quickly and therefore helps prevent them from mixing. For these types of drinks, the order is important. It is much more difficult to layer a heavier ingredient on top of a lighter one.

LAYER OVER ICE—Fill the glass with ice and gently pour each ingredient in so that they mix as little as possible.

LAYER OVER ICE. DRINK THROUGH A STRAW—Layer the drink over ice as described above, but add a straw. These types of drinks are meant to be consumed quickly, with the layers of the drink providing different flavors.

POUR INGREDIENTS INTO THE GLASS NEAT (DO NOT CHILL)—Add all of the ingredients into the glass (typically a shot glass) straight from the bottle. Don't chill them if they're not already cold.

SHAKE WITH ICE AND STRAIN—This technique requires either a cocktail shaker or a Boston shaker. Fill the cup of the shaker with ice, add the ingredients, and cover it with the lid. Shake it briskly until the outside begins to frost. Then take the top lid off (for a cocktail shaker) or remove the pint glass and place the strainer over the cup (for a Boston shaker) and strain the drink into the glass, leaving the ice behind in the shaker. This is the common method for creating a martini.

SHAKE WITH ICE AND STRAIN OVER ICE—This is the same as shaking with ice above. The difference is that the glass is filled with ice before you strain the drink into it.

SHAKE WITH ICE AND POUR—This is the same as shake with ice above but you

remove the strainer and allow the drink to pour into the glass with the ice.

SHAKE ALL BUT X WITH ICE AND STRAIN INTO THE GLASS. TOP WITH X—In this case, X is typically club soda or tonic water. It can also be ginger ale or even champagne. Shake all the ingredients in a shaker with ice and strain them into a glass. Then fill the glass the rest of the way with X. Whether or not to add ice to the glass before straining in the drink depends on the type of drink. If ice would dilute the mixer (champagne for example) then ice should not be added.

STIR GENTLY WITH ICE AND STRAIN—Using a cocktail shaker or a Boston shaker, combine the ingredients and ice. This time, instead of shaking them, stir them gently with a bar spoon before straining the mixture into the appropriate glass.

STIR GENTLY WITH ICE—Using a cocktail shaker or a Boston shaker, combine the ingredients and ice. Stir them gently with a bar spoon and pour them into the glass.

STOCKING A HOME BAR

*

Stocking a home bar depends on many factors: The tastes of those who will partake, the space you have available, and, of course, the amount of money you're willing to spend. Based on my experience, you can keep most people happy with a few basic liquors, liqueurs, wine, and a small assortment of beers.

THE BASICS

*

BOURBON—Wild Turkey, Maker's Mark, and Jim Beam are among the biggest names.

GIN—Use recognized brands like Tanqueray, Gordon's, or Bombay Sapphire.

RUM—Here you might want at least three different types: a dark (Gosling's Black Seal or Myers's), a light (Bacardi), and a spiced rum (Captain Morgan).

SCOTCH—Scotch can easily get expensive. Choose according to the tastes of your guests and your budget. Cutty Sark, Johnnie Walker, J&B, and Teacher's are among the most well known. If your guests appreciate a good whiskey, then a single malt scotch might be called for.

TEQUILA—There are two different types of tequila drinkers. There's the "lick it, slam it, suck it" crowd (based on the traditional salt, shot, lime sequence) and

there is the 100% blue agave sipping crowd. To keep both happy, consider a bottle of Jose Cuervo for the slammers and a more upscale tequila such as Patrón or XQ for the sipping crowd.

VODKA—Typically, a premium name brand such as Absolut or Skyy will please everyone. You can make it more upscale with super-premium vodka such as Grey Goose.

WHISKEY—Good whiskey can get expensive. For some, a basic bottle of Jack Daniel's might suffice, while for others you might want an assortment of Irish, Canadian, and American whiskies. It's up to you.

Liqueurs

*

There are literally hundreds of different liqueurs and liquors out there in almost every flavor.

Brandies—Flavored brandies are often a party favorite, especially with older guests. The common ones are cherry and blackberry.

Crèmes—The essentials here are crème de menthe (green and/or white), crème de cacao (brown or white), and crème de banana.

Orange-flavored Liqueurs—There are many different kinds of liqueurs flavored with orange. They are often lumped together under the name triple sec, but they include items such as Grand Marnier, blue curaçao, and Cointreau.

Schnapps—The single most commonly used schnapps in the United States is peach schnapps. It's used in everything from Sex on the Beach to the Woo Woo. After peach, you might want to consider melon (Midori), apple, butterscotch, or any other flavors that strike your fancy.

Others—Kahlúa, Jägermeister, Rumple Minze, Bénédictine, Frangelico, and Chambord are some common staples as well.

Wine

*

Billy Joel said it best: "Bottle of red, bottle of white, whatever kind of mood you're in tonight."

When it comes to wine, mild-mannered people become freakish snobs. You'll never please everyone, so it's best to keep it simple with a good bottle of merlot

and a nice chardonnay. Wine doesn't keep well after it's opened, so trying to keep a large selection on hand is not really practical. Of course, if you know that your guests like a particular style (say a fine Mad Dog 20/20 or a good vintage Wild Irish Rose) then you should base your wine offerings on your guests' tastes.

BEER

*

With beer, as with wine, it depends on the tastes of your guests. Typically for a large party, I'll have a lot of Corona and Coors Light and a small selection of others such as Samuel Adams, Beck's, Budweiser, and a few cans of Guinness.

If you don't know your guests tastes ahead of time, then you'll need a selection that includes domestic and imported beer, as well as at least one brand of light beer. You might want to consider a nonalcoholic beer as well.

There is also a new trend in the category of "Clear Malts." Zima was the first, but they now seem to be everywhere: Smirnoff, Skyy, and Bacardi each have a clear malt, premium-flavored beverage out. I've tried all three and like Skyy Blue the best. But, of course, a twelve-pack of Skyy Blue costs more than a case of Corona!

Mixers

✳

Mixers are almost as important as the liquors themselves. Here are the basics that will satisfy almost any guest. One thing to keep in mind is that sodas will go flat over time, even if the bottle is never opened. This is especially true of club soda and tonic water. As a general rule, if the bottle is more than six months old, consider replacing it.

Cola—Coca-Cola or Pepsi—I get whatever's on sale.

Cranberry Juice

Diet Cola—Some prefer Diet Coke, some, Diet Pepsi, and others like Pepsi One. I try to keep them all on hand.

Ginger Ale, Tonic Water, and Club Soda—Unless you use them all the time, get small bottles so less is wasted.

Grapefruit Juice

Orange Juice

Pineapple Juice—This is available in little eight-ounce cans and keeps for years, so it's easy to keep it available without it going bad.

Sprite / 7-Up

BAR MIXES

✳

BLOODY MARY MIX—I've never been asked for a Bloody Mary in my entire career. But you never know.

GRENADINE

LIME JUICE

MARGARITA MIX—Pick your favorite. It beats squeezing limes.

SOUR MIX—You can buy this at most grocery stores in either a bottle or in a powder. You can also make your own with lemon juice, sugar, and water.

GLOSSARY OF INGREDIENTS

*

Below is a description of some of the ingredients used in this book. Several Internet sources were used to produce these definitions, including the Internet Cocktail Database (cocktaildb.com) and various product and company websites.

ABSINTHE—A high-proof (50–75% alcohol by volume) anise-flavored spirit made from several herbs and flowers, including the flowers, and leaves of the *Artemisia absinthium*, also known as wormwood. Sale of absinthe was banned in most of the world between 1907 and 1915.

ADVOCAAT—A creamy Dutch liqueur made from a blend of brandy, herb extracts, sugar, vanilla, and egg yolks. The drink started in the Dutch colonies in South America, where it was made from avocados. When the drink was brought north, egg yolks replaced the tropical fruit.

AGAVERO—A tequila-based liqueur made from a blend of tequila and damiana flowers. The liqueur is very sweet, with a strong agave flavor.

ALIZÉ—A French brand that offers several varieties of cognac and fruit juice blends. The original flavor of Alizé (Alizé Gold Passion) is a blend of French vodka and passion fruit juice.

AMARETTO—An Italian liqueur made from apricot kernels and seeds and almond extract steeped in brandy and sweetened with sugar syrup. *Amaretto* is Italian for "a little bitter." The two best-known brands are Disaronno Originale and Lazzaroni. In addition to these, there are amaretti made by the large distilleries, including Bols, DeKuyper, and Hiram Walker.

Amaro Averna—An Italian herbal liqueur based on a secret recipe created in Caltanissetta in 1854. The liqueur has a mild bitter flavor and is used as a digestive in Italy.

Amarula Cream Liqueur—A cream liqueur made in South Africa from the fruit of the African marula tree.

Anisette—An Italian anise-flavored liqueur mainly consumed in France and Spain. It is sweeter than most anise-flavored liqueurs (such as pastis or Pernod), and also has a lower alcohol content (typically 25% by volume, versus 40%).

Aperol—An Italian aperitif made of an infusion of neutral spirits with bitter orange, gentian, rhubarb, and an array of herbs and roots using a secret recipe that has been unchanged since its first creation in 1919. It has a sweet-bitter orange and herbs taste and a red-orange color.

Applejack—An alcoholic beverage produced from apples that originated during the American Colonial period. It is made by concentrating hard cider, either by the traditional method of freeze distillation, or by true evaporative distillation. The term "applejack" is derived from "jacking," a term for freeze distillation.

Aquavit—A caraway-flavored liqueur from Scandinavia. Its name comes from *aqua vitae*, Latin for "water of life."

Armagnac—A brandy similar to Cognac produced in the Armagnac region of France. Armagnac differs from Cognac in that it's only distilled once instead of twice. The distillation also occurs at a lower temperature, allowing more of the character of the fruit to remain.

B&B—Bénédictine that has been diluted with brandy, making it less sweet. The product is made by the same people that make Bénédictine, and it was introduced in the 1930s to offer the drier taste that people seemed to prefer at the time.

Bärenjäger—A German neutral spirit–based liqueur that is sweetened and then flavored with honey. The word translates as "bear hunter."

BÉNÉDICTINE—A brandy-based herbal liqueur produced in France. Bénédictine is believed to be the oldest liqueur continuously made, having first been developed by Dom Bernardo Vincelli in 1510, at the Bénédictine Abbey of Fécamp in Normandy. Every bottle of Bénédictine carries the initials "D.O.M.", which stand for "Deo Optimo Maximo," or, in English, "To God, most good, most great."

BITTERS—Bitter-tasting herbal flavorings. Originally marketed as patent medicines, the few remaining varieties are principally used as a flavoring in food recipes or in cocktails.

> **ANGOSTURA BITTERS**—Angostura was named for the town of Angostura in Venezuela. It contains no angostura bark, a medicinal bark which is named after the same town. Angostura Bitters is the most widely distributed bar item in the world.

> **PEYCHAUD'S BITTERS**—Peychaud's is associated with New Orleans, Louisiana, and can be difficult to find elsewhere. It has a subtly different and sweeter taste than the Angostura brand.

> **ORANGE BITTERS**—Made from the rinds of unripe oranges.

CURAÇAO—A liqueur flavored with the dried peels of Larahas, bitter relatives of oranges, grown on the island of Curaçao. The liqueur has an orange flavor and is packaged with various coloring added. The most common color is blue, but it is also sold in green, orange, and red colors.

BOURBON—An American form of whiskey made from at least 51% corn, with the remainder being wheat or rye and malted barley. It is distilled to no more than 160 proof and aged in new, charred, white oak barrels for at least two years. It must be put into the barrels at no more than 125–U.S. proof; in this way it is similar to scotch whisky, which is also aged in charred barrels.

BRANDY—An alcoholic spirit distilled from wine. The name comes from the Dutch word *brandewijn*, which means "burnt wine."

CALVADOS—A French spirit made from distilled apple wine. The American version, known as applejack, is similar in flavor.

CAMPARI—A branded alcoholic beverage (between 20–24% alcohol by volume) introduced in Italy in 1860 by Gaspare Campari. It is a mild bitters-type aperitif, often drunk with soda, orange juice, or in mixed drinks.

CHAMBORD—A French liqueur made from small black raspberries.

CHAMPAGNE—A sparkling wine produced only in the Champagne region of France. Champagne is produced by adding sugar to bottled wine, which allows additional fermentation to occur in the bottle, producing carbon dioxide bubbles.

CHARTREUSE—A famous herbal French liqueur still produced by the Carthusian monks in France from a formula dating back to 1605 and containing 130 herbs and spices.

> **GREEN CHARTREUSE**—55% alcohol by volume and naturally green in color. The color chartreuse is named after the liqueur.

> **YELLOW CHARTREUSE**—Only 40% alcohol by volume, it has a milder and sweeter flavor.

CLAMATO—A trademark of the Mott's company for a drink composed of a blend of tomato juice and clam broth.

COGNAC—A type of brandy that is produced only in the Cognac region of western France and is universally recognized as the finest and most elegant liqueur in the world. Not a drop of any other wine or brandy is ever allowed to enter a bottle of Cognac.

COINTREAU—A fine, colorless, orange-flavored liqueur made from the dried skins of curaçao oranges grown on the island of the same name in the Dutch West Indies. The generic term is *curaçao*, and if redistilled and clarified is called triple sec.

COURVOISIER—A type of cognac. Courvoisier is famous for being the favorite drink of Napoléon.

CRÈME LIQUEURS—Crème liqueurs are very sweet, with a single flavor that dominates.

> **CRÈME DE ALMOND**—Almond-flavored.
>
> **CRÈME DE BANANA**—Banana-flavored.
>
> **CRÈME DE CACAO (DARK)**—Chocolate-flavored and dark brown in color.
>
> **CRÈME DE CACAO (WHITE)**—Chocolate-flavored but colorless.
>
> **CRÈME DE CASSIS**—Black-currant flavored.
>
> **CRÈME DE COCONUT**—Coconut-flavored.
>
> **CRÈME DE MENTHE (GREEN)**—Mint-flavored and green in color.
>
> **CRÈME DE MENTHE (WHITE)**—Mint-flavored but colorless.
>
> **CRÈME DE NOYAUX**—Made from fruit pits, with a bitter almond flavor.
>
> **CRÈME DE VIOLETTE (OR CRÈME YVETTE)**—Made from and flavored with violets.

CREAM SODA—A vanilla-flavored carbonated soda.

CREAM SHERRY—A style of sweet sherry created by blending dry sherry with sweet wines. The result is a dark, rich wine with a soft, sweet finish.

CROWN ROYAL—A brand of blended Canadian whisky.

DRAMBUIE—A famous whisky liqueur consisting of Highland malt scotch whisky, heather honey, and herbs.

DUBONNET—A brand of quinquina, a sweetened, fortified apertif wine that contains quinine. Produced in France, it comes in two varieties.

> **BLONDE**—Lighter in color and less sweet.
>
> **ROUGE**—Red in color and more sweet.

EVERCLEAR—A brand of grain alcohol 95% alcohol by volume (190 proof).

FERNET-BRANCA—An extremely bitter Italian herbal apertif or digestif made from cinchoma bark, gentium, rhubarb, calamus, angelica, myrrh, chamomile, and peppermint. It is often employed as a stomach settler and/or hangover remedy. It's classified as bitters.

FIRE WATER—A brand of cinnamon-flavored liqueur that is bright red in color.

FRANGELICO—An Italian brand of hazelnut-flavored liqueur packaged in a distinctive monk-shaped bottle.

GALLIANO—A sweetish, golden, Italian liqueur with an herby, spicy taste.

GIN—Gin begins as a neutral spirit. It is then redistilled with, or filtered through, juniper berries and botanicals such as coriander seed, cassia bark, orange peels, fennel seeds, anise, caraway, angelica root, licorice, lemon peel, almonds, cinnamon bark, bergamot, or cocoa. It is this secondary process that imparts to each gin its particular taste.

> **DRY (OR LONDON DRY) GIN**—Most of the gin now produced is London dry, which is light, dry, and perfect for making martinis and other mixed drinks.

> **PLYMOUTH GIN**—A sweeter and milder gin originally produced in Plymouth, England.

GINGER BEER—A type of fermented, carbonated beverage flavored with ginger, lemon, and sugar. Ginger beer reached the height of its popularity in England in the 1900s. It is popular today in Bermuda and is part of the "national drink" of Bermuda, the "Dark 'n' Stormy." Jamaican-style ginger beer adds capsaicin, the flavor that gives peppers and hot sauces their heat, which makes for a very different flavor of ginger beer.

GODIVA LIQUEUR—A neutral spirit–based liqueur flavored with Godiva brand Belgian chocolate and other flavors. There are currently three types: dark chocolate, white chocolate, and milk chocolate.

GOLDSCHLÄGER—A cinnamon-flavored liqueur produced in Switzerland that includes flakes of real gold in the bottle.

GOSLING'S BLACK SEAL RUM—A brand of rum produced on the island of Bermuda. The rum is dark, sweet, and the main ingredient in a Dark 'n' Stormy, the official cocktail of Bermuda. The rum was originally bottled in champagne bottles sealed with black wax, giving it its name.

GRAIN ALCOHOL—Un-aged neutral spirits with a very high alcohol content (greater than 90% alcohol by volume or 180 proof). Grain alcohol cannot be legally sold in many states in the United States.

GRAND MARNIER—A French brand of aged orange-flavored liqueur (triple sec) with a brandy base.

GRAPPA—An Italian brandy distilled from the pulpy mass of skins, pits, and stalks left in the wine press after the juice of the grapes has been extracted. Young grappa can be harsh, but it mellows with age.

GRENADINE—A sweet syrup flavoring for drinks, made from pomegranate juice, containing little or no alcohol.

GUINNESS STOUT—A dry stout made from water, barley malt, hops, and brewer's yeast. A proportion of the barley is flaked and roasted to give Guinness its dark color and characteristic taste. Draught and canned Guinness both contain nitrogen in addition to the natural CO_2. The nitrogen in the beer is part of what gives Guinness its thick head and "waterfall" settling effect.

HARD APPLE CIDER (OR HARD CIDER)—Fermented apple cider with an alcohol content similar to beer.

HEERING CHERRY LIQUEUR—A proprietary Danish cherry liqueur with a brandy base that has been produced since 1818 under several different names, including "Heering," "Peter Heering," and "Cherry Heering."

HENNESSY—A brand of cognac produced in France by James Hennessy and Co. and the Hennessy family. The Hennessy company produces more than twenty different brands of cognac and is considered the largest cognac producer in the world.

HOT DAMN! CINNAMON SCHNAPPS—A brand of cinnamon-flavored liqueur with a strong flavor and a red color.

HPNOTIQ—A French fruit liqueur made from vodka, cognac, and tropical fruit juices.

IRISH CREAM LIQUEUR—A mocha-flavored whiskey and double-cream liqueur, made with a combination of Irish whiskey, cream, coffee, chocolate, and other flavors.

IRISH MIST—A liqueur produced in Ireland, consisting of Irish whiskey flavored with heather honey.

JACK DANIEL'S—A whiskey made in Tennessee; it is perhaps the most famous whiskey made in America. The Jack Daniel's distillery in Lynchburg, Tennessee, dates from 1875 and is the oldest registered distillery in the United States. Jack Daniel's is made according to the sour-mash process and by the "Lincoln County Process" of filtration through sugar maple charcoal before being aged in charred American oak casks.

JÄGERMEISTER—A complex, aromatic liqueur containing some fifty-six herbs, roots, and fruits that has been popular in Germany since its introduction in 1935. In Germany it is frequently consumed warm as an apertif or after-dinner drink. In the United States, due to some savvy marketing by the importer, it is widely popular as a chilled shooter.

KEKE BEACH LIQUEUR—A key lime–flavored cream liqueur with a hint of graham cracker flavor as well.

KIRSCHWASSER—A clear brandy made from double distillation of the fermented juice of black cherries.

KÜMMEL—A sweet, colorless liqueur flavored with caraway seed, cumin, and fennel.

LICOR 43 (CUARENTA Y TRES)—A yellow-colored liqueur from Spain. It is made from fruit juices, vanilla, and other aromatic herbs and spices. There are forty-three different ingredients that are used, hence the name.

LILLET—An aperitif wine from the Bordeaux region of France. Lillet is sold in both red and white.

LIMONCELLO—An Italian liqueur made from lemons.

MADEIRA—A fortified wine made in the Madeira Islands of Portugal and popular as a dessert wine or for cooking.

MALIBU RUM—A Caribbean coconut-flavored rum liqueur.

MANDARINE NAPOLÉON LIQUEUR—A liqueur made from mandarin orange–flavored cognac.

MARASCHINO—A very sweet white cherry liqueur made from the Marasca cherry of Dalmatia, Croatia. This liqueur is sometimes used in sours in place of sugar.

MARSALA—A fortified wine made in the Italian city of Marsala. It is traditionally served chilled with a spicy cheese between the first and second course of a meal or warmed as a dessert wine. It is also used for cooking.

MELON LIQUEUR—A pale green liqueur that tastes of fresh muskmelon or cantaloupe. The most famous brand, Midori, is Japanese in origin and produced by the Suntory Company in Mexico, France, and Japan.

METAXA—A strong, sharp-tasting, aromatic Greek brandy.

MEZCAL—A Mexican-distilled spirit made from the agave plant. Tequila is a mezcal made only from the blue agave plant in the region around Tequila, Jalisco. Spirits labeled "mezcal" are made from other agave plants and are not part of the tequila family.

MOONSHINE—A term used to describe high-proof, un-aged, distilled spirits. Other terms include white lightning, mountain dew, hootch, and white whiskey. *Moonshine* once only referred to spirits made illegally but has recently been used to describe craft-distilled un-aged liquor that has been produced by licensed distilleries.

MUSCATEL—A wine, often fortified, produced from the Muscat variety of grape.

NASSAU ROYALE—A rum-based liqueur with a vanilla flavor.

OUZO—An anise-flavored liqueur from Greece, usually served on the rocks. Ouzo can be used as a substitute for absinthe in many cases.

PARFAIT AMOUR—A cordial made of citrus juices, cinnamon, coriander, and brandy.

PASSOÃ—A passion fruit–flavored liqueur produced by Rémy Cointreau.

PASTIS—A semisweet anise-flavored liqueur produced to be a substitute for absinthe without the wormwood.

PEACH SCHNAPPS—A sweet peach-flavored liqueur.

PERNOD—A popular brand of pastis produced by the Pernod Ricard company.

PISANG AMBON—A Dutch liqueur, green in color and flavored with banana.

PISCO—A brandy produced in the wine-producing regions of South America. It is the most popular spirit in Chile and Peru.

PONCHE KUBA—A "ponche" is a homemade cream liqueur similar to eggnog that is popular in Caribbean and Latin American countries. Ponche Kuba is a packaged form of this liqueur. It is made from a rum base, with cream, eggs, and sugar added. It's flavored with a proprietary blend of spices.

PORT—A sweet, fortified wine from the Douro Valley in the northern part of Portugal.

RED BULL—A carbonated soft drink with additives and extra caffeine that are supposed to reduce mental and physical fatigue.

ROCK & RYE—A blend of rye whiskey with rock candy and fruit juice.

RUM—A liquor made from fermented and distilled sugar cane juice or molasses. Rum has a very wide range of flavors from light and dry, like a vodka, to very dark and complex, like a cognac.

> **AMBER RUM**—Gold in color and sweeter than a light rum.
>
> **AÑEJO RUM**—A rum that has been aged in wood for a period of time.
>
> **DARK RUM**—Dark, almost black in color, with a rich and complex flavor.
>
> **FLAVORED RUMS**—Like vodka, rum is now available in a wide array of flavors. Some of the first flavored rums featured vanilla or lemon. Now, almost any flavor can be found.
>
> **LIGHT RUM**—Clear in color and dry in flavor.
>
> **RUM CREAM**—Cream liqueurs made with a rum base, with cream and flavoring added. The flavors are typically tropical, such as banana, coconut, and pineapple.
>
> **SPICED RUM**—The original flavored rum. Spiced rum consists of an amber rum with vanilla and cinnamon flavor added.

RUMPLE MINZE—A 100-proof (50% alcohol by volume) peppermint schnapps produced in Germany.

SAFARI—A fruit liqueur flavored with mango, papaya, passion fruit, and lime.

SAKE—A Japanese alcoholic beverage brewed from rice. It is commonly referred to as "rice wine" in the United States, but, because of how it is produced, it has more in common with a malt liquor.

SAMBUCA—An Italian liqueur flavored with anise and elderberry. It is produced in both clear ("white sambuca") and dark blue or purple ("black sambuca") versions.

SCHNAPPS—A liqueur distilled from grains, roots, or fruits. Real schnapps has no sugar or flavoring added, as the flavor should originate from the base material. Many syrupy sweet fruit liqueurs are being called schnapps. These are not true schnapps because they have both sugar and flavorings added.

SCOTCH—Scotch whisky is whisky that is produced in Scotland. In the United States this whisky is commonly referred to as Scotch. In Scotland, however, it is referred to simply as whisky.

SHERRY—A type of wine produced in Spain that is fortified with brandy.

SIMPLE SYRUP (OR SUGAR SYRUP)—A combination of equal parts sugar and boiling water, allowed to cool and bottled as a sweetener in many mixed drinks.

SLOE GIN—A liqueur flavored with sloe berries and blackthorn fruit. It was traditionally made with a gin base with sugar added. Most modern versions use a neutral spirit base and add flavorings later.

SOUTHERN COMFORT—A liqueur with a neutral spirit base and peach and almond flavors.

STOUT—A beer made with roasted barley or malt. The roasting of the grain gives the beer a darker color and a stronger flavor.

STREGA—An Italian herbal liqueur with mint and fennel flavors. Saffron in the recipe gives it a yellow color. *Strega* is Italian for "witch."

SWEET & SOUR MIX—A syrup made from a blend of sugar and lemon juice. A simple recipe is to mix equal parts of simple syrup and lemon juice.

SWEETENED LIME JUICE—As the name would imply, lime juice with sugar added.

TABASCO SAUCE—A brand of hot pepper sauce made from a blend of Tabasco peppers and vinegar and salt aged in wood casks.

TANG—An orange-flavored powdered drink mix brand owned by Kraft Foods. It was introduced in 1959, but became popular when NASA gave it to astronauts in the 1960s.

TEQUILA—A type of mezcal that is made only from the blue agave plant in the region surrounding Tequila, a town in the Mexican state of Jalisco. Tequila is made in many different styles, with the difference among them mostly dependent on how long the distillate has been aged before being bottled.

    ANEJO—Aged between one and three years.

    GOLD ("ORO" OR "JOVEN ABOCADO")—Meaning "bottled when young," this is white tequila with coloring added.

    REPOSADO ("RESTED")—Aged at least one year.

    SILVER ("PLATA" OR "BLANCO")—This is clear, un-aged tequila. It has a very strong flavor.

    TEQUILA ROSE—A brand of cream liqueur with a tequila base and a strawberry flavor.

TIA MARIA—A brand of coffee-flavored liqueur from Jamaica. Tia Maria is Jamaican rum–based and flavored with spices.

TONIC WATER—Carbonated water with quinine added. Originally used to prevent malaria, the amount of quinine in bottled tonic water today is only about half of the dose given to patients.

TRIPLE SEC—A highly popular flavoring agent in many drinks, triple sec is the best-known form of curaçao, a liqueur made from the skins of the curaçao orange.

VERMOUTH—A fortified wine flavored with aromatic herbs and spices. There are three common varieties of vermouth.

    DRY VERMOUTH—Clear or pale yellow in color and very dry in flavor.

    SWEET VERMOUTH—Red in color and sweeter.

    WHITE VERMOUTH—Clear or pale yellow in color but sweeter than dry vermouth.

VODKA—A neutral spirit that can be distilled from almost anything that will ferment (grain, potato, grapes, corn, and beets). It is distilled multiple times and filtered to remove as many of the impurities as possible. It is then diluted with water to bring the alcohol content down before being bottled. Vodka is also found in a wide variety of flavors, from bison grass to watermelon.

WASABI—A member of the cabbage family, the root is ground and used as a very potent Japanese spice.

WHISKEY (OR WHISKY)—A beverage distilled from fermented grain and aged in oak casks. The location, grain, type of oak, and length of the aging time all affect the flavor of the whiskey. Whisky is spelled with an "e" in Ireland and the United States and without the "e" everywhere else. There are four major regions where whiskey is produced: Ireland, Scotland, Canada, and the United States. Each has a different style that imparts a distinctive flavor.

WILD TURKEY—A brand of Kentucky bourbon whiskey. It is available in both 80-proof and 101-proof versions.

WINE—An alcoholic beverage produced by the fermentation of fruit juice, typically grapes. The type of grape, where the grapes were grown, and the way the wine is stored as it ferments affect the taste and color.

YUKON JACK—A Canadian liqueur made from a whiskey base and flavored with honey.

RECIPES

———————— ✳ ————————

CREDITS

---✳---